MOVING DAY

by Harold T. Rober

LERNER PUBLICATIONS ◆ MINNEAPOLIS

Note to Educators:

Throughout this book, you'll find critical thinking questions. These can be used to engage young readers in thinking critically about the topic and in using the text and photos to do so.

Lerner Publications Company
A division of Lerner Publishing Group, Inc.
241 First Avenue North
Minneapolis, MN 55401 USA

For reading levels and more information, look up this title at www.lernerbooks.com.

Library of Congress Cataloging-in-Publication Data

Names: Rober, Harold T., author.
Title: Moving day / by Harold T. Rober.
Description: Minneapolis : Lerner Publications, [2016] | Audience: Ages 4–8. | Audience: K to grade 3. | Includes bibliographical references and index.
Identifiers: LCCN 2016018697 (print) | LCCN 2016020019 (ebook) | ISBN 9781512425512 (lb : alk. paper) | ISBN 9781512429299 (pb : alk. paper) | ISBN 9781512427479 (eb pdf)
Subjects: LCSH: Moving, Household—Juvenile literature.
Classification: LCC TX307 .R63 2016 (print) | LCC TX307 (ebook) | DDC 648.9—dc23

LC record available at https://lccn.loc.gov/2016018697

Manufactured in the United States of America
1 – VP – 12/31/16

Table of Contents

Time to Move

It's time to move!

Moving to a new home can be fun.

Moving can also

be scary.

People say good-bye

to friends.

It can make them

feel sad.

Why could moving to a new home be scary?

The family packs their things.

They use bubble wrap so nothing will break.

They put everything into boxes.

What else could you wrap things in so that they don't break?

People put the boxes

inside a big truck.

They use a dolly

for heavy things.

dolly

The family goes to their new home.

It looks different from their

old home.

They take the boxes out of the truck. They carry the boxes into the new home.

It is time to unpack.

People find new spots

for things.

The family walks around the new neighborhood.

It is fun to meet new neighbors.

Why is it fun to meet new neighbors?

The kids go to a new school.

They make new friends!

Moving Supplies

bubble wrap

Picture Glossary

bubble wrap

plastic with air inside to cushion objects

dolly

an object with wheels that is used to move heavy objects

neighborhood

an area where people live

unpack

to take things out of boxes

Index

Read More

Blevins, Wiley. *I'm Not Moving!* South Egremont, MA: Red Chair Press, 2015.

McMillan, Sue. *Moving Day.* New York: Parragon, 2011.

Petersen, Christine. *The Smart Kid's Guide to Moving.* Mankato, MN: Child's World, 2014.

Photo Credits

The images in this book are used with the permission of: © vgajic/iStock.com, p. 5; © szefei/iStock.com, pp. 6–7; © wavebreakmedia/Shutterstock.com, pp. 8, 16–17, 23 (top left), 23 (bottom right); © kali9/iStock.com, pp. 10–11, 23 (top right); © Monkey Business Images/Shutterstock.com, p. 12; © Andresr/Shutterstock.com, p. 15; © Kali Nine LLC/iStock.com, pp. 18, 23 (bottom left); © Pressmaster/Shutterstock.com, p. 21; © Mike Flippo/Shutterstock.com, p. 22 (right); © chrisbrignell/iStock.com, p. 22 (bottom left); © Rob Wilson/Shutterstock.com, p. 22 (top left).

Front Cover: © Darren Baker/Shutterstock.com.